The

No Good

LEADER

Phill C. Akinwale

The No Good Leader

Published by Praizion Media

P.O. Box 22241, Mesa, AZ 85277

E-mail: info@praizion.com

www.praizion.com

Author: Phill C. Akinwale

Illustrator: Leo Lätti

Editors:

Catherine Van Herrin

Phyllis Akinwale

ISBN 978-1-934579-42-8

Printed in the United States of America

Table of Contents

"At the end of the day, the most overwhelming key to a child's success is the positive involvement of parents."

Jane D. Hull

Chapter 1: Proud Parents

"Look at him; he has your eyes…"

"And your beak…"

Peedy and Sweetie just couldn't help but coo as they gazed down at their just-hatched little chick, his eyes staring up at his parents in wide-eyed wonderment.

"I know, good thing he didn't get your mother's—boy, does *she* have a honker."

"Peedy!" Sweetie squawked as she gave her husband a playful nip on the tail feathers.

"Sorry, hon, but I call 'em as I see 'em! Speaking of which. . .what should we call him?"

The little **chick** gazed from one parrot parent to the other, in anticipation.

"Hmmm. . .I think we'll name him. . .'Needy,' said Sweetie. "'Needy?'" Peedy squawked so loud, he could be heard a mile away. "No son of mine will be named 'Needy,' and that's the end of it!"

"Why not? It rhymes with Peedy and Sweetie."

"Sweetie, you know I love you, but are you nuts? Can you imagine what he'd have to endure in life with that name? We'll call him 'Meedy.'"

And so it was settled. The newly named Meedy gave a little tweet of approval and snuggled beneath his father's wing. "Yes, that's my son!" he announced with final approval. "Meedy, I will teach you everything you need to know to be a good, kind and successful Parrot, and you will make your Mom and I very proud," he proclaimed.

"Now it's time to let the rest of the flock know," Peedy said, releasing the boy to his mother. Peedy grabbed a claw-full of special sunflower seed sticks he had been saving for just this occasion, and fluttered off as proud as an eagle, shouting, "It's a Boy!" while dropping the sticks off at every nest in the neighborhood to squawks and squeals of delight and congratulations.

"Parents wonder why the streams are bitter, when they themselves have poisoned the fountain."
John Locke

Chapter 2: Meet the Eeedys

P eedy stuck to his word.

He made sure he taught his young hatchling about their distinctive parrot family lineage. "The Eeedy Parrots have always been great leaders and innovators," Peedy proudly told Meedy as they walked past a long line of portraits that hung on one side of their tree wall.

"Here's your great-great-Grandfather, Henree Fordeedy, who invented the first assembly line to mass-produce sunflower sticks," he said, pointing to the smartly dressed Parrot in the elegant frame, "or this one, your uncle JP Greetty, who found a way to get fuel oil out of seeds," he added. Peedy understood the importance of family heritage and ancestry, and wanted to instill it in his son early in his life. "And this is Mario Andreedy, the champion race car driver," he continued as they moved down the line.

Wow, thought Meedy to himself, *such great parrots, every one of them! How will I ever live up to a reputation like that?* "And you, too, Dad, don't forget—everybody loves you at the Seed Plant," Meedy piped up.

"Who, me? Well, thanks, Meedy," Peedy said with a modest chuckle. "I do a good job, and I like it very much, but I am just a mid-level quality control specialist. But you, my boy, are destined for something greater. I see it in you already," Peedy said, gesturing towards the Eeedy Family Wall of Fame. "Just always remember our family creed. . ." he began.

"Birds of a feather flock together?" asked Meedy, interrupting.

"No, said Peedy smiling, "Fly as if you are an eagle, laugh like a kookaburra, love like a dove, be as good as a goose, and proud as a peacock, and you will be one perfect parrot!"

"Okay, Dad, I promise," Meedy said, giving his father his best one-winged salute.

"And I promise to do everything I can to help you," Peedy said, proudly patting his boy on the head.

Over the years, Peedy made good on that promise. He arranged for Meedy to get the very best education any young parrot could receive. He graduated at the top of his class from the Emperor Penguin's School for Birds, where he tutored and mentored younger chicks, and he even received a special community service award for his Anti-Bullying program. He attended the prestigious Maltese Falcon Academy high school, where he was val-egg-dictorian and continued his good works, taking seeds to homeless pigeons in the park every weekend.

After that, Meedy went on to Massachusetts Polly Tech on a full bird scholarship, where he graduated suma squawk-louder, with an MPA—Master's in Parrot Administration. And finally, here he was, ready to start as

Assistant Seed Counter in the Actuary Department of the very same seed plant where his father worked.

"Look at you – just look at you, my boy, all grown up," Peedy said grasping Meedy firmly by his shoulders. "And so strong too."

Meedy said, "I'm going to make you proud, Dad. I am going to be a great leader, kind and generous and thoughtful. . .just like our creed."

"Uh, yeah, about that," Peedy said, looking over his wing to make sure no one was listening, "You know, son, a lot has changed since your grandfather's days, especially around here." Peedy said, scuffing his claws along the dirt floor like a bull about to charge. "Now you have to scrape and claw to get ahead."

"But Dad, you said. . . ."

"I KNOW what I said," Peedy squawked wildly, "but that was then, and this is now! And now, in the real world, nice guys finish last! Just look at me, kid—I'm in the same old office doing the same old job that I was when you were born more than twenty years ago! But I said it then, and I'll say it again now." Peedy again grasped his son's shoulders and stared deeply into his eyes, full of pain and tears in his own, "You can do better. You ARE better. You just have to let them know that, each and every day. If this job has taught me anything, the people who work for you are beneath you—just little branches for you to step on as you swing up by beak and claw to the top of the tree!"

"I don't know, Pop, that's not the kind of thing they taught me in ethics class at Polly Tech. . . ."

"Forget what you learned in school, Son, and listen to me!" Peedy bellowed. All my mentees are VPs and C-level executives. McStingy was but a lad when I showed him the ropes here but now he is the Chief Executive Officer. So much for being nice! He has kept me here in this lowly position; I can barely make ends-meet. Listen! I'm your Father, and I only want what's best for you!"

Meedy left his father's office that day feeling very hurt and confused. But, because he trusted and respected his father, he followed his advice. He became ruthless, ruffling many feathers as he clawed his way to the top.

Soon, around the water coolers and in hushed tones in the breakroom, the others in the seed factory started referring to him as "Greedy Meedy." He heard about this from his assistant, a smallish lizard named Ms. Gecko, who was shocked when, in response, he turned to her and said, "Greed is good, Ms. Gecko."

In less than four years, he became the company's youngest department head, and just one year after that, he became Senior Manager of Shelling and Shucking, pulling in six figures, more than 100,000 seeds a year!

"The only time some people work like a horse is when the boss rides them."

Gabriel Heatter

Chapter 3: A Day in the Office

"**D**on't just stand there Parker!

Come in, come in, I haven't got all day you know!"

Parker the parakeet was the shift Floor Supervisor; he hated it when Meedy summoned him. He shuffled into his boss's luxurious office with trepidation.

"What is it? Cat got your tongue?" Meedy clucked menacingly.

"It's, it's, this memo, Sir," Parker said as Meedy swiped the paper out from Parker's beak. "It says that you now want all workers on the line to shuck shells only with their left claws."

"So?"

"Well, last week, you issued a memo directing them to only use their right claws."

Meedy leaned over his desk, his imposing frame dwarfing Parker's. "I know. And have you seen these numbers!" Meedy said, spinning his computer monitor around to Parker with his beak. "I am not a pleased parrot! I want to see if they can do better with their left claws."

"But they haven't been trained to use their left claws!"

"That's not my problem, is it, Parker? And besides, we both know that we are ambidextrous!"

"Ambi-what, Sir?" Parker said, cowering a little.

"AMBIDEXTROUS! You fool, don't you eat with your right foot as well as with your left?"

"Yes, but. . ."

"No, buts, Parker – those are for humans, not parrots. Left claws it is, and you had better hit over 20,000 units this week, or your tail feathers will be in a sling!"

Later in the executive cafeteria, Meedy met up with his Department VP, Deevly. "I tell you Deeve, old boy, you should have seen his face when I told him to switch the line workers from their right claws to the left—I thought he was going to leave a dropping right there in my office!"

"It's like I told you, Meedster; always keep them guessing—keep them off balance. The less they know about your playbook, the better!" Deevly said as he grabbed two sunflower martinis from the wet bar. As he loudly slurped his drink from his dark tongue, he said, "You'll go far in this company—I can just taste it!" The pair made their way over to a table.

"So what are you going to do next, make them switch back over to the right claw again?" Deevly asked with a devious twinkle in his eye.

"Oh, I have something even better than that in mind," Meedy replied as he clinked glasses with his boss.

Meanwhile, things were a mess on the shucking floor. The workers were giving it the old team try, being as optimistic as they could be, but despite their remarkable dexterity, they were having a hard time getting used to working in the opposite direction, and seeds were flying all over the place. The line just kept overflowing—it was as though, Pandora had opened her box!

But back at the cafeteria, Meedy and Deevly were finishing up their gourmet lunch of macadamia nut tar-tar and mango soufflé. "So how's the family, Meed? I hear you have a chick on the way."

"Twins, in fact; yeah, they should hatch any day—and none too soon—man, has the wife been impossible these last few weeks!"

"Ah, come on, little Tweedy? She's one of the sweetest birds I know, and cute too!"

"Hey, watch it! And you just wait till it's Leely's turn; nothing can turn a chickadee into a condor quicker than having to squat on a couple of eggs for a month!"

Later, Meedy was back in his office playing "Angry Humans" on his computer when Ms. Gecko's voice came through the speakerphone. "Yes, Ms. Gecko, what is it? I am very busy at the moment!"

"I'm here with Ms. Dovey for our 2:30 appointment."

"Here with who? For what?"

"Ms. Dovey, the new hire in Accounting you wanted to meet," replied Ms. Gecko.

"Oh yes, yes. . .come on in," Meedy said quickly, clearing the game from his screen.

Ms. Gecko entered the office along with a very beautiful white dove.

"Ladies, please come on in, sit down." Meedy gazed up and down at Ms. Dovey, hardly hiding his admiration of her perfect form. "My, my, my, aren't you the pretty bird. It's about time, Gecko. The last few you brought in here were real dogs!"

As Ms. Gecko fluffed up in anger, Dovey bowed her head in embarrassment and said very timidly, "Mr. Meedy that is not very nice language."

Meedy laughed, "No, I mean they were *real* dogs. . . paws, not claws, and couldn't shuck shells for beans! Anyway, nice to meet you," Meedy said, extending his wing. Dovey shook it but felt he held on a little too long, which made her squirm on her perch even more uncomfortably.

He released Dovey's wing and turned to Ms. Gecko. "So, Gecko, you know my wife is about to have hatchlings, and lately she has been a real. . . .

"Mr. Meedy!" Ms. Gecko said, cutting him off.

"Well, a real you-know-what. Anyway, Gecko, why don't you pop over to one of those fancy foo-foo stores you chickpeas like and pick her up something nice and frilly for me to take home to her tonight."

Ms. Gecko replied indignantly, "Mr. Meedy, I have told you before, I am your personal assistant for business matters only, and it is not in my job description to go shopping for your wife!"

Dovey looked like she was trying to find a space to crawl into to hide.

Meedy puffed himself up. "And when I ask an employee to do something for me, to pick up the ball and help me out, that's what I call teamwork. And teamwork is in everybody's job description," he said hotly, turning to look directly at the cowering Dovey. "Isn't that right, Ms., Ms. . . . ."

"Dovey, it's Dovey," she tweeted nervously.

"Ah, yes, 'Dovey'. . .and what a Lovey Dovey you are," he said. Snapping out of his reverie, he again turned to Ms. Gecko.

"Gecko, why are you still here? Are you going to cooperate, or must I look for a new real team player?" he said while staring deliberately at Dovey.

Ms. Gecko bowed her head and said dejectedly, "Yes, Sir."

"Good! Here's a few dollars, now go and pick out something pretty. And you, Dovey, welcome to the team, and be sure to walk out very slowly when you leave." He chuckled so hard, he snorted in delight.

Poor Dovey literally became even whiter than a dove and just barely managed to walk out in utter shock.

"The corporation is the "master", the employee is the "servant". Because the corporation owns the means of production without which the employee could not make a living,

the employee needs the corporation more than vice versa."

Peter Drucker

Chapter 4: Family Matters

A few days later, Meedy was in his office.

He was going over some notes with Ms. Gecko, when a canary began pounding loudly at his window.

"Excuse me Ms. Gecko, it looks like I have an urgent "tweet" coming in." Meedy flung the window open. The canary settled down onto his desk and chirped, "Honey, it's time. Come home quick."

"Oh my! Gecko! Cancel all of my appointments for the rest of the day." He said to the little bird, "Tell her I'm on my way." The canary took off like a shot, back out the window.

Meedy pulled a bunch of sunflower sticks out of his top drawer, shoved one in Ms. Gecko's mouth, and said, "I'm going to be a father! Congratulate me, Gecko, and hand the rest of these out!" Then he quickly fluttered off after the canary.

Meedy arrived at home just in time to see the first of his twin chicks poke its beak through its egg. After a few more little pecks, a little parrot with colorful tail-feathers popped out with a soft "peep."

"It's a boy!" squawked Meedy. Seconds later, he was joined by another, this one with pink tail-feathers.

"And a girl!" Squealed Tweedy even louder.

Meedy and Tweedy nuzzled each other's necks and then gathered their children between their wings.

Tweedy rubbed beaks with the girl and said, "Your name will be 'Eeedy,' just like your father's sister."

Meedy held his newborn boy gently and said, "And you will be Beedy, named after your great uncle. I will teach you everything you need to know to be a good, kind and successful parrot, and you will make your Mom and I very proud."

Just as he finished saying those words, Meedy thought they sounded strangely familiar, and for some reason, he felt sad for a moment. But he quickly dismissed the thought, figuring he was just caught up in the excitement of the moment.

The next morning, Tweedy was already feeding the chicks, when Meedy came downstairs. Tweedy was very surprised to see him dressed for work.

"What are you doing?" she asked in disbelief.

"Going to work, what does it look like I'm doing?"

"I can see that," her ire rising, "but don't you think they can do without you for a day? You just became a father!"

"It looks like you have things well in wing. . ."

Tweedy began to cry. "You know, when you were born, your father took a leave of absence for almost a month to be with you and help your mother!"

"And that's why my father, The Great Parrot, rest his soul, never amounted to anything more than a middle manager, and I grew up in that stinky little tree on the other side of town."

Meedy gestured all around him. "Look at this, look what you have—a mighty fine six-nest-room split-level oak, with all the modern conveniences. What do you think pays for all this? These kids, *my* kids, are going to have everything they need!" he shouted as he flew out of the tree.

"'Everything'? Really!" Tweedy squawked after him. "I don't think so!" And she continued sobbing, wondering what had happened to the parrot she had fallen in love with.

Back at work, Meedy was looking over the reports from Parker. He would chew him out later for it taking so long to get the workers up to speed on left-handed shucking, but for now, he was going to have to answer to his big boss, the CEO of the Surly Seed Company, a stuffy old barn owl, named Mr. McStingy.

As if on cue, Ms. Gecko yelled through on his speakerphone. "Mr. McStingy wants to see you in his office right away."

Meedy made the trek to what the rest of the workers called "The Cage" somewhat reluctantly. He didn't like having to answer to anyone, but he grudgingly waddled up the steps to McStingy's office, tightening his neck feathers as McStingy's secretary ushered him inside.

The short, heavy-set owl looked him in the eye, "Come in, Meedy, have a perch, have a perch. Heard you just became a dad. Congratulations. I have four, or is it five, myself. No matter. Glad you are back here on the job, where you belong. Never understood that 'parrotically correct' nonsense about 'Family Leave' for fathers! Leave the women's work to the women, I always say!" He chuckled to himself.

"I couldn't agree with you more, Sir."

"Good. So I am sure you have seen the reports of this week's quota. Quite dismal, I must say."

"Well, you see, Mr. McStingy, Parker was supposed to. . ."

"Parker is an idiot!" McStingy interrupted, just like his father was. If he wasn't my wife's nephew, I'd have fired him a long time ago. Look, Meedy, I spoke with Deevly. I know what you were trying to do with that switcheroo, but now what do we do to make up for it?"

"Well, I actually did have a plan all along, Sir. You see, first I got them to shuck with their right claws. . ."

"Yes?"

"And then their left claws. . ."

"Uh huh."

"So now we'll make them shuck with both claws at the same time! They can work twice as hard and shuck twice as many seeds in the same shift!"

"Brilliant, my boy! Absolutely brilliant! And now that they can work with both claws, we'll have to make up for the time lost while they were learning how to do it. Put everyone on double shifts this week. They will pull in their quotas and then some."

"Right you are, Sir, and after the little wringer I just ran them through, they'll be glad to get the overtime."

"Overtime?" McStingy said, raising his voice. "Whoooooooo said anything about overtime? Is fatherhood making you go soft on me, Meedy?"

"No, Sir, I mean, I just thought. . ."

"Just thought what?" McStingy said, staring down at Meedy with his huge owl eyes.

"Nothing, Sir. I'd better go ask Parker to tell the floor about the double shifts."

"Good. You'll go far in this company, Meedy."

"Don't blame the boss.

He has enough problems."

Donald Rumsfeld

Chapter 5: Drive 'Em Hard!

"**Y**ou, you can't be serious!"

"Shuck seeds with both claws, and work a double shift, with no overtime? I'll have a revolt on my claws!"

"Any worker who complains, Parker, will be sent home immediately and will not be welcomed back. Please make sure that is clear," Meedy told his incredulous foreman. "And if anybody calls in sick or complains of clawple-tunnel syndrome, I'll be sure to cut their health benefits, is that understood?"

Parker just stood there, his head bowed in shock and disbelief.

"I SAID, 'Is that understood, Mr. Parker?'"

Parker managed to squeak out a weak, "Yes, Sir."

"Don't look so sad, Parker. You have to get the line workers to respect you; do you want to be a lowly foreman parakeet all your life? I'm trying to make a parrot out of you!"

Parker kept his head down and muttered weakly, "I'm not sure that's what your father would have said being a parrot was all about."

"What? What was that about my father? What do YOU know about my father, anyway?"

Parker looked up. "My father worked with your father. He said Peedy was the finest Parrot he ever knew. He was kind. He knew all about great leadership and project management. He helped the workers meet their quotas by showing them ways to work smarter, not harder, and he was never cruel. All the workers loved him. . ."

"SHUT UP!" Meedy squawked. "You don't know anything about my father! He was weak! And that was why he never got anywhere! Now get out of here before I make it TRIPLE shifts!"

Meedy was very shaken. As soon as Parker left, he went over to the bar and mixed a stiff drink.

"Am I grumpy? I might be. But I think maybe sometimes it's misinterpreted."

Harrison Ford

Chapter 6: Discovering the Past

Eventually, many months later…

…. the workers at the plant did get the hang of double handed shucking, but it was very hard work, and the better they got at it, the higher McStingy's quarterly bonus from the board became and the higher he raised the worker's quotas.

Meedy's workers did their jobs not out of respect, but for fear of Meedy. It was a very uncomfortable work environment for everyone, Meedy included. He was becoming increasingly paranoid about his own position in the firm, constantly afraid that someone was gunning for his job. Unfortunately, that sinking feeling only made him ride Parker and the line workers much harder. The tension was taking its toll at home, as well, and Meedy's drinking was spiraling out of control.

"Tag, you're it!" Eeedy slapped her brother on the back and flew off at full-tilt.

"Not if I can help it!" Beedy replied as he zoomed around the kitchen in a flurry of feathers.

"What's all this racket!" Meedy croaked as he came down the stairs, looking very haggard.

"Aww, we were just playing, Dad. And besides, it's Saturday! No school, whoopee!" Beedy said, and again zoomed around the kitchen.

Meedy staggered slowly to the coffee pot and poured himself a cup. "Well, take it outside then; I have a headache.

I had a rough night."

"You seem to be having a lot of them lately," Tweedy chimed in.

"And just what is that supposed to mean?" Meedy asked his wife snarkily.

"Nothing. It just seems to me that lately, I go to bed, and you stay up, maybe drinking a little too much..."

Meedy snapped at her, "What I do at night, and how much I drink is my business no one else's!"

Sensing one of Meedy's all too frequent rages coming on, Tweedy turned to her chicks and said, "You know what, kids, your father's right, why don't you go outside and play for awhile."

"Aww, Mom," they said in unison, but something in their mother's face told the young birds that she was right, and they flapped off outside.

Meedy took a sip of coffee. "Ah. . .that's the ticket. I guess I'll go up and get dressed now."

"Dressed? Dressed for what?"

"For the office, what else?"

"For Polly's sake, Meed, it's Saturday, and you promised the kids you would help them make costumes for their school play today!"

"Costumes. . .for a school play? That's what you expect me to do when I have McStingy over me all the time, and that young buck in Picking and Packing, what's his name, Bambi, nipping at my claws for my job?"

"Oh come on, Meedy, shucking has always been run by a parrot. Now you are really worrying me. . . do you seriously think a deer wants your job?"

"Okay, maybe I am being a little paranoid, but I am still going in today, and that's that!"

A few moments later the chicks came back. Upon entering the tree Beedy said, "Hey, mom, wussup, did I just see Dad leaving, dressed for work?"

"Yeah, what's going on?" Eeedy inquired. "Daddy said he was going to help us with our costumes today!"

"It's okay, kids, I know what he promised, but you know, his work is very important. . ."

"Yeah, I'll say, more important than us," the twins said dejectedly.

"Now, you know that is not true. Daddy loves you both very much; it's just that things at work are very tough right now, and. . ."

"I wish Daddy didn't have that stupid job!" Eeedy interrupted.

Tweedy sighed, "You know, honey, sometimes I wish that, too, but, hey, come on, let's make the best of it. I'll lead the way to the attic."

In the attic, Beedy found a huge carton. He opened it and exclaimed, "Hey, look, there's lots of neat stuff in here, check this out." He pulled out a sleeveless black T-shirt, emblazoned with a hip-looking logo, and as he did so, a picture fell from the folds of the shirt and fluttered to the floor.

Eeedy picked up the picture. It was a photo of a rock band, and the parrot in the front at the microphone was wearing the T-shirt.

"Look at this!" Eeedy squeaked with delight. "It's a picture of an old rock band!"

Her mother and brother came over to look and saw the band's name emblazoned across the drum kit: "The Flying Stars"

Tweedy quickly snatched the picture away from her daughter's grasp. She put her wing to her mouth and said, "Oh – my – gosh. . ." as tears began to well up in her eyes.

"What, what is it, Mom? Eeedy asked. "Who's that in the picture?"

Tweedy stammered, "Th-that's your father, in the club, when I first met him."

"Dad was in a rock band? No way!" said Beedy.

"Yes, yes he was. And he was very good, too." Tweedy went over to the carton Beedy had opened and began digging through it.

"Look, here's his guitar." Beedy picked it up and strummed it.

The chords seemed to take Tweedy back in time.

"So what happened, Momma?" her daughter's words shook her from her daydream.

Tweedy closed the flaps on the box. "Oh, well, we started to get serious, and your grandfather, well, he didn't think being a musician was any way to raise a family, so he got your father his first job at the Seed Plant. Dad kept playing for a while, not professionally or anything, just for fun, and for me. But then he got promoted at the plant, and one thing led to another, and this stuff just ended up here, tucked away in a box like a distant memory. . .just like. . .just like. . ." she began to cry.

Eeedy and Beedy put their wings around their mother. "It's alright, don't cry, Momma," said Eeedy reassuringly.

"Yeah," added Beedy, "maybe Daddy will play the guitar for you again someday."

"I know! We'll ask him to!" the chicks said together.

Tweedy sniffled and smoothed out her feathers. "No, I don't think that's a very good idea. Here, give me that," she said, gesturing to the guitar. "Let's put that back in here and look for those costumes, okay, guys?"

"That was it, that was the last straw."

Thomas Carter

Chapter 7: The Last Straw

Meedy's problems at home continued to worsen.

So did his drinking. No longer committed to putting in extra time at the office, since he spent most of his weekends sleeping off major benders, it was all he could do to get to work on time during the week. His increasingly poor performance did not go unnoticed.

"Sorry, Sir, you can't come in here," the burly hawk said to Meedy as he attempted to enter the Executive Cafeteria.

"Whaddya mean, 'Sorry, Sir?' It's me, Harley, let me through!" Meedy squawked at the Seed Company's head security guard, who continued to bar his way.

Meedy tried to go around him, to no avail. "What, what's going on here? Don't you know who I am anymore?" Meedy squawked indignantly.

"Yes. Yes, I do, Sir."

"Well, this is the Executive Cafeteria, isn't it?"

"Yes. That it is, Sir," Harley the Hawk replied stoically.

"And I am an executive of this firm, aren't I?"

"Indeed you are, Sir."

"So? Let me in!"

"I am sorry, Sir, but your privileges have been revoked."

"Revoked! Revoked by whom?"

"I am not at liberty to say, Sir."

Behind the guard, Meedy saw Deevly sitting at the bar and shouted out to him. "Hey! Deevly! What gives? Tell this avian blockhead to let me in!"

Deevly just ignored him.

"Sir. Calm down," said Harley.

"Hey, Deevly, I am talking to you, buster. Hey, man, come on, it's me, Meed!"

"Sir, if you do not stop shouting, I will have to take further action."

"You are going to what? Oh, come on, this is just ridiculous!" And with that, Meedy tried to push past the hefty Hawk. In a flash, Harley had Meedy with his wing twisted painfully behind his back, his body pointing away from the cafeteria entrance. Meedy started squawking very, very, loudly, and all eyes in the cafeteria turned towards him. Finally, Deevly put down his drink, excused himself and said to his guest, "I've got this."

When Meedy saw Deevly walking toward him, he immediately calmed down. "Nice, Deeve, real nice. Okay, joke's over. Come on, tell this guy to let me go, and let's have a drink!"

Deevly folded his wings behind his back and looked at Meedy very seriously. "It's no joke, Meedy. Now, please, leave—you are embarrassing me and yourself in front of some very important clients."

"Huh, what? What's this all about, Deeve?"

"Not here. Not now. My office in one hour, got that?"

"What are you talking about, Deeve?"

Deevly looked at Harley, who twisted Meedy's wing even harder.

"OUCH!"

"I said, my office, one hour!" The guard began to exert a little more pressure.

"Yeah, yeah, okay, Deeve, I got it, your office, one hour."

"Good." The guard eased off a little. "Harley, my business with Mr. Meedy here is concluded. Please see him safely back to his office." He turned and walked briskly back into the cafeteria while the mighty Hawk unceremoniously escorted Meedy back to his office.

An hour later, Meedy stormed into Deevly's office, still fuming.

"Okay, Deevly, you want to tell me what in the egg that was all about back there?"

"Sit down, shut up, and listen. What I did back there was for your own good. Just be thankful I got you out of there before McStingy showed up for our meeting, or you'd be out of here for sure, and forever!"

"Meeting, what meeting? What are you talking about?"

"Do you know who I was entertaining at the bar during your little fiasco? That was Petey, as in Petey's Pecans and Pralines. We were talking about a merger. McStingy was on his way to meet us for lunch to start to hammer out the details. Do you know how huge a deal a merger between Surly Sunflower and Petey Pecan can be? We will corner the entire nut and seed market. Your little show back there didn't help any," he huffed.

"I'm, I'm sorry, Deeve, I really am. I didn't know."

"Why should you know? When were you at the last Executive Board Meeting?"

"I don't know, you know, things have been kind of tough at home, with the kids and all. . .so I've been late a couple times, maybe missed a meeting or two, so what?"

"Well, I *do* know. You haven't made it in on time for a meeting since last month. You've already been in late four times this month, and it's only the 10th. That's why I had to revoke your lunch privileges. Listen, I am on your side here, Meed. I always have been. But the Old Man is getting really ticked. What is up with you lately anyway, dude?"

"I don't know, Deeve. It used to all be so clear to me. But lately, I don't know, everything seems to be coming apart here, at home, everything. . ."

"Well, you need to get it together, and quick. Straighten up and fly right, or I don't think I can help you anymore."

Later, Meedy was in his office, still a bit rattled by the incident at the cafeteria and his conversation with Deevly, when he realized it was time for his meeting with Ms. Dovey to go over the quarterly reports. He smiled. Oh, well, at least he still looked forward to that. He always enjoyed his meetings with Ms. Dovey, even if he rarely remembered what they spoke about after she left, as he was unable to concentrate on little else but her exquisite form.

"Come in, come in, Lovey Dovey, so nice to see you again. How is my favorite little chickee today?"

Dovey heaved a heavy sigh at his vile language. She just wanted to do her job and get out of his office. She despised the way Meedy leered at her and spoke to her, but he was the boss, and getting work wasn't easy.

When Dovey sat down, Meedy said, "Oh, would you please get my copy of the report? I left it on the credenza behind you." As she turned around, he gave her a playful little pat on her tail feathers.

Dovey whirled around at him, furious. "That is the LAST STRAW, Mr. Meedy!" She got right up in his beak. "I am not, and have never been your 'Little Chickee,' and I have had enough of this harassment!"

"Harassment? Come on, I'm just having a little fun."

"Fun? Fun, Mr. Meedy? Do you think it's 'fun' to have you and every other male bird in this company staring at my tail feathers every time I walk down the hallways as if it's mating season? I expect that from some of the workers, but I thought better of you." Her voice continued to rise, and Meedy slowly backed away from her.

"I am not a Chick, a Chickee, a Chickadee, a Chippy or a Chirpy. . .and I most certainly am NOT your 'Lovey Dovey.' In fact, you can be sure I will be filing a complaint with Avian Resources about this! Good day to you, SIR!" she said as she stormed out of his office.

Meedy nervously thought it was time to beat a hasty retreat. "Ah, Ms. Gecko, something has come up at home. I need to take the rest of the day off," he squeaked into the speakerphone and quickly flew out the back door.

The next day, as soon as he arrived at the plant, again late, Ms. Gecko greeted him outside his office. "McStingy has been bellowing for you all morning. He wants you in his office *now*!"

Meedy trembled; he knew this could not be good.

"Come in, Meedy. Close the door behind you, please," the old owl began matter-of-factly.

"Meedy, you know I am a bird of few words. So I will come right to the point. You're fired. Please pack up your personal items and go."

"But, Sir. . ."

"No buts, you are lucky you are only being fired and not brought up on charges of sexual harassment. The Board was able to smooth things over with Ms. Dovey. What the egg were you thinking? Didn't you know she is the

Chairman's godchild? Not to mention how such a suit would have tanked the Pecan merger?"

Meedy begin to open his beak to talk, but McStingy cut him off.

"NO, Meedy, there is nothing more to say; you are done here." He turned to his intercom. "Harley, please come to my office and see that Mr. Meedy picks up his personal belongings and is escorted from the building."

"I didn't see it then, but it turned out that getting fired from Apple was the best thing that could have ever happened to me.

The heaviness of being successful was replaced by the lightness of being a beginner again, less sure about everything.

It freed me to enter one of the most creative periods of my life."

Steve Jobs

Chapter 8: Personal Issues

Weeks went by.

Meedy's downward spiral went from bad to worse. He couldn't find work in the seed business after being blacklisted by McStingy. He was increasingly belligerent to his wife and kids, and increasingly drunk. On the day the last unemployment check came in, Tweedy had no choice but to confront her husband.

"Meedy, you know I love you, and I have always stood by you. I am not sure how we came to this, but now we have to do something. Now, I need to get the kids off to school. I understand you can't get work in the industry, but somehow you need to put seed on the table!"

After Tweedy left, Meedy again looked unsuccessfully through the classified ads, and he suddenly had a desperate idea. He went up to the attic to look for some boxes of odds and ends. He grabbed what he wanted and began sewing and taping furiously. When he finished, he looked in the mirror. "There. . .not bad, I think a make a pretty good pigeon."

He planned to go down to The Square at the park, where the humans were always throwing seeds to the pigeons. But as he walked towards the stairway down from the attic, something on the floor caught his eye.

He bent down and picked up the old, long-forgotten picture of himself playing with the Flying Stars. A tear welled up in his eye. He stashed the picture in his pocket.

At the park, Meedy found that being a pigeon was not so easy. It was very crowded. The humans seemed to have some of their own particular favorites who always got the seeds. Though he tried to elbow his way through the crowds, he was the lowest bird on the pecking order, and all of these park pigeons were well practiced at getting fed. He was about to give up when he saw a pigeon standing by himself, away from the rest of the crowd. He made his way over to him.

"You sure don't look like no pigeon I ever saw, Son," the lone bird said to Meedy.

"That so, Old Timer? Well you don't look like the usual bums I see around here, either."

"That is because, Sir, I am not your 'usual bum.'" The pigeon puffed out his chest with pride, which Meedy could now see was adorned with a cluster of medals. "You are in the presence of an Officer, Sir. Colonel Flap, Retired, 1st Carrier Pigeon Brigade." The Colonel snapped Meedy a sharp salute. "Served this country proudly for three tours, but ever since they came up with all that digital communications gear, there hasn't been much use for us Carrier Pigeons any more. So here I am retired and helping a new generation of pigeons to find their way to success. So what's your story, boy? As I said, you sure don't look like a pigeon."

"I'm not a pigeon," Meedy said, taking off his makeshift headgear. "I'm a parrot."

"A parrot?" said the Colonel in disbelief. "What's a bird like you doing in a place like this?"

"You know what, Colonel, I really wish I knew. A year or so ago I could have bought this entire Square, and now here I am, begging in it."

"Hard times can fall on anyone, Son, nothing to be ashamed of. Come here, you look like you could use a pick-me-up. I've been saving this for a special occasion, got it from a human the other day."

The Colonel took out a juicy chocolate-covered peanut. "Here, have a bite," he said as he gave it to Meedy, who took a little nibble.

"Wow! That's delicious! What is it? Hey, wait a minute. . .I feel kinda strange." Meedy started swaying back and forth, as if he were drunk. "Colonel, Colonel, I feel weird. . ." Meedy was trying to focus on the Colonel, but now he could see two, then three of him, and his voice sounded like it was coming from a well way off in the distance.

"Son, Son, speak to me, are you okay? It was just a chocolate-covered peanut, pigeons love 'em, and I thought it would make you feel better."

"CHOCOLATE!" Meedy squawked, "I'm a parrot, I told you! Parrots can't have chocolate, it's poison to us. . ." And with that, Meedy passed out.

When Meedy finally awoke, he wasn't in The Square anymore. He was in a beautiful, lush green garden by a babbling brook. "Hey, I know this place!" He took a deep breath. "I know the smell of this grass." He spun around, dropped to the ground and started rolling around playfully. He popped up, "I know that brook! This is Hobsgarden!" he exclaimed as he started running toward the brook. "This is the place I used to go worming with DAD!"

And there he was, Meedy's father, Peedy, who had just plucked a huge worm from the ground by the brook and swallowed it back. "Hiya, Son, come on over, the worms are as good as ever!"

"Dad, is that really you? Am I, am I. . .dead?"

"Not yet. Not quite, anyway," Peedy said. "Let's just say you're a step higher than the Land of Nod. Which means that maybe, just maybe, I can give you something a lot better than my last bit of advice."

"What's that, Dad, what can you give me?"

"A second chance. You see, Son, when I told you all of that stuff about forgetting the family creed and being mean and nasty to get ahead," Peedy said, bowing his head in shame, "I was wrong, Son, very wrong. I was just bitter about my own life and how I ended up. I guess I felt I never lived up to the standards of our ancestors."

"But Dad, I never thought little of you. I loved you. And I thought it was so great how everybody at the plant loved you, too! When I was growing up, I wanted to be just like you!"

"I know that, and that's what I was afraid of, boy. I didn't want you to be just like me; I wanted you to be *better*, so I filled your head with all that nonsense. But it's not too late, Son—you can still be better than me; you can be a great leader, but the right kind of leader, like our forebears. It's not too late for you."

"What do you mean, Dad? What should I do?"

Peedy smiled. "Fly like an eagle, laugh like a kookaburra, love like a dove, give as good as a goose, and be as proud as **a** peacock, and you will be one perfect parrot! Oh, and listen to the Colonel—he's a wise old bird."

"The Colonel?" Peedy's image seemed to be wavering, becoming more and more distant as he spoke. . . .

"Yes, goodbye, Son. . . ."

"...SON! Can you hear me, boy? Come on back." The Colonel was furiously performing CPR on Meedy when suddenly the parrot's eyes flung open. "DAD!"

"No, not quite, but boy, you had me scared there for a moment!"

Meedy looked around. He was back in the Square.

"Colonel, you brought me back!"

"Saw my share of young boys almost buy it in the war. Couldn't save 'em all. But guess I remembered enough of my medic training to help you." The Colonel turned to leave.

"Help me? YES, that's right, you can help me! Teach me, Sir. Teach me how to be a great leader."

The Colonel turned back. "A great leader, you say? You know what, Son," the Colonel pointed to his chest. "Ya see this medal? They gave it to me 'cause I brought twenty-six boys from our unit back out from behind enemy lines under heavy fire. They said I was a 'great leader.' Try telling that to the mothers of five boys who didn't make it."

Meedy just cocked his head to the side, not really understanding.

"I never meet a great leader who started out wanting to be one. They just wanted to be the best they could be, for their friends, their colleagues, their families, their country, and especially themselves. The leader thing? That just came later. Now, if you just want to be a leader just to rise to the top—and I suspect that's how you wound up here, down at the bottom; then I can't help you. But if you want to find what it takes to be a better Parrot, the kind that can lead himself to greatness and the kind anyone would gladly follow, well, come along then, we've got a lot of work to do!"

The two new friends flew back to the Colonel's coop. The walls were lined with more medals and citations. Meedy's eyes stopped on one in particular.

"Wow, Colonel, the Medal of Valor, that's our country's highest honor! You *are* a great leader. I can never be as brave as you!"

"Brave? Do you think it was brave charging up that hill to save my men? Do you want to know the bravest thing I had to do? When I got back and went to the families of each of those five men that I lost to personally tell them how sorry I was. That was the hardest thing I had to do. They may not hand out medals for that kind of courage, but that is the first thing you are going to do. You are going to say you are sorry, and mean it, to that young lady you insulted, and to your foreman, who you rode so hard, and most especially, you need to say sorry to your wife and family."

Meedy thought about those words and the words of his father, and he realized that he had made one real idiot of himself. But he suddenly felt a sense of hope from the Colonel—maybe it wasn't too late to change!

"Now come on over here, Boy, we are going to learn about what really makes a great leader." The Colonel spread out a bunch of books, biographies mostly, across the table.

"You know what all of these birds had in common? Before they became great leaders, they knew what it meant to be team players. They understood and practiced the laws from the human leadership guru John C. Maxwell; his Law of the Inner Circle and his Law of Addition! They rose to the top not by stepping on the people below them, but by being a rising tide that lifted all boats. They understood the Law of Addition and what it really meant to add value to others and equip them for success. They didn't hide their knowledge; whoever told you that was a real bozo!"

Meedy smiled at that as he thought about Deevly.

"No, Meedy, real leaders share their knowledge with others willingly. Their subordinates appreciate it and often find ways to build on it, and then everyone does better!"

Meedy nodded in understanding.

"And I'll tell you another thing you'll find as you read about those men and women—they all did something they really loved to do," the Colonel continued assuredly.

Meedy began poring over the books, reading the histories of the great leaders, and finding wisdom and power in their words.

One quote he particularly took to heart was one from a great human leader, Steve Jobs, who said, *"Management is about persuading people to do the things they do not want to do, while leadership is about inspiring people to do the things they never thought they could."*

Meedy also liked this one, by another human, General Douglas MacArthur: *"A general is just as good, or just as bad as the troops under his command make him."*

Another favorite, was from a lady, Eleanor Roosevelt: *"A good leader inspires people to have confidence in the leader, a great leader inspires people to have confidence in themselves."* And that was the beginning of Meedy's lengthy lesson in leadership under the Colonel's mentorship.

Meedy also found himself drawn to quotes on self development from BC Forbes.

Finally, a quote that made him reflect on his family from another human, Bill Gates: *"I'm serious when I do my work. I'm not serious when I'm home with my kids."*

The Colonel left Meedy alone for hours a day to read over his library of books until one day Meedy stumbled on a gold colored hardback book in the library.

The gold colored book glowed mysteriously in the Colonel's dim-lit library in an almost supernatural way. Full of curiosity, Meedy opened the book and then...he saw the title: *12 Steps to Leadership Infinity by Phill C. Akinwale*

"Hmmm, another human," he thought. And with that thought he flipped the weathered pages eagerly to the first introductory section which read:

A TRUE LEADER LEADS HIMSELF FIRST TO REALISE DREAMS AND GOALS BEFORE LEADING OTHERS.

12 Steps to Leadership Infinity: The Unending Spiral

By Phill C. Akinwale

Reflections on Your Leadership

i. Think about your life.

ii. What intangible assets have you?

iii. What skills and gifts do you have?

iv. When you look back, would you say that you have been a good custodian of your skills and abilities?

v. Have you been a good leader?

vi. Have you invested time, energy and resources in developing your skills and honing in on your God-given skills and abilities?

vii. Have you effectively and passionately led yourself to success?

viii. Are you daily leading yourself on a path to success or are you wallowing in failure, doom and gloom?

ix. Can you truly say you are a good leader? Or a NO GOOD leader?

x. Are you ready to commit time to learning how to lead yourself more effectively?

Am I a Leader?

A leader is someone who through innovation, influence and the guidance of a carefully selected team transforms resources – both tangible and intangible – knowledge, skills, ideas, tools, facts, techniques, technology and assets into a desired end goal, result, product, service or some other measurable outcome.

Self Leadership

Self-leadership is the ability to lead oneself, motivate and inspire oneself to achieve a definite end goal. Napoleon Hill calls this a definite chief aim.

In order to lead yourself effectively, you must clearly and articulately list out your definite chief aim. This could be a definite chief aim that could take a period of days, weeks, months or years to implement.

Your definite chief aim ultimately takes you closer to your life ambition. What is your life ambition?

If you had the opportunity to be something, be someone new or do something phenomenal, what would you like to be? Who would you rather be and what would you rather do?

Your definite chief aim should align with these goals and desires. Do not be caught living life as the wrong person! You do not want to live for someone else's dream. Live for yours!

Great self leadership involves leading yourself with inspiration, innovation and conviction towards your goals. Great self-leadership ensures the effective management of your available talents, skills, ambitions, drive and resources (both tangible and intangible) to achieve one's definite chief aim. Let's examine these leadership enablers one by one.

Innovation

An innovative leader can creatively think, identify unseen needs and take action in uniquely transferring or converting needs, ideas and resources into a result never before conceived.

A true leader thinks outside the box. Sometimes being innovative simply means using what is already available to create something entirely new or never before imagined in that form.

No sooner had Meedy read the first page of the book, his eyes popped wide open and thought about all his skills and longtime ambitions that had once lived in his heart so passionately. He wondered where his love for music and people had gone and what he could do with his talents. "I have not been a great leader of my abilities. I was really good back in the day." He thought.

Meedy began day-dreaming of himself on a huge stage playing his guitar and singing to a cheering audience of boys and girls, men and women when suddenly a booming voice snapped him out of his imaginary world.

"WELL MY BOY! DID YOU LEARN ANYTHING ABOUT HOW TO BE A GOOD LEADER?" boomed Colonel's voice through the hallway into the library.

"Yes Colonel" said Meedy grinning. "I really learned a lot. Things not entirely new but I think my leadership faculties are actually unlocked and activated for the very first time! I guess I kind of already was cut out for this stuff, I just was so lost along the way somewhere."

"Son, what do you think learning is? Most of the time it's just being reminded of what we already know." Said Colonel.

Meedy snapped shut the *12 Steps to Leadership Infinity*. "Thank you, Colonel, I've got a lot do! And I promise you I'll do it. But may I ask one last favor?"

"Sure" said Colonel.

"*12 Steps to Leadership Infinity*? May I return it when I am done studying it or when I can afford to buy one?"

"Keep it safe!" demanded Colonel. "It's the only copy in the world! A personal gift from the author."

"Wow!" exclaimed Meedy. I promise to keep it safe! I learnt a whole lot from the first page alone!"

"You got yourself a deal youngster! See you around!" soon said Colonel.

Meedy flew off, and as he did for a minute there, the Colonel thought his old eyes were playing tricks on him, because he could have sworn it was an eagle, and not a parrot, that had just flown his coop.

"Think not of yourself as the architect of your career but as the sculptor. Expect to have to do a lot of hard hammering and chiseling and scraping and polishing."

Bertie Charles Forbes

Chapter 9: New Beginnings

Meedy made good on his promises to the Colonel.

He did go back and apologize to Ms. Dovey, and to Parker, Deevly, McStingy and all of the line workers.

McStingy was so impressed he even offered him his job back, but Meedy declined. The old owl opened his eyes wide as Meedy took a picture out of his pocket, looked at it and said, "I thank you, Sir, but there was always something else I wanted to do."

Meedy sobered up and became the ideal husband and father. He took a job as a seed boy at a record company. He started at the bottom, but he didn't care. He brought seeds to the performers during and in between their recording sessions, filled their water, and swept up seed shells after the sessions. He was always kind to his co-workers, clients, and anyone who visited the studio. He was well-liked and respected by everybody in the company.

One day during the recording for an album that was to be a fundraiser for a major charity event, the lead guitarist in the band suddenly hit a very sour note.

"Cut!" yelled the sound engineer.

"Hey dude, what is it, man? That sounded gnarly," said the lead singer.

"Don't know, Ace, it's my wing, it hurts like crazy. I can't play."

Mr. Shreembly, the producer, burst into the sound booth. "Can't play? What do you mean, he can't play? I have some of the biggest VIPs in the city waiting for these tracks at a major black-tie premier in one hour! If we don't show up with the discs, we'll be ruined!"

Meedy heard all this as he was sweeping up shells in the back of the studio. He put down his broom, came forward and said, "Excuse me, Sir, but I think I can play the guitar track. I have been listening to every one of their sessions for weeks!"

Shreembly said, "Meedy, you are probably one of the best workers I have, a real team player, and I know that you want to help, but you're a shell boy, you are no guitar player."

"Well, actually, Mr. Shreembly, I do play. . .a little."

The guitarist said, "Hey, man, give him a chance, what have we got to lose? Here, dude, take my axe." And he handed the guitar to Meedy.

Meedy played the track perfectly and even added an impromptu solo lick that blew the producer and the sound engineer away! The record took off like wildfire, sales went through the roof, and it was the biggest hit the record company ever had.

Because of the way he stepped up to the task, Mr. Shreembly promoted Meedy to Operations Manager. Soon he became VP of Sales and Marketing, all the while remembering the lessons he had learned in the Colonel's coop and the book *12 Steps to Leadership Infinity*.

He still found time to play and record, and eventually cut a record with the reformed Flying Stars.

The record went to number one! Meedy took the proceeds from the album, and started his own company, which offered a unique music therapy program for recovering alcoholics. Everyone in the company felt he was the most remarkable CEO they had ever worked for. He became a major philanthropist, funding many charities, not the least of which was The Meedy Home For Veteran Carrier Pigeons, and he visited its most decorated resident, the Colonel, there very often.

But of all the things he did to make good, especially whenever he was with Beedy, Eeedy and Tweedy, was to, fly as if he was an eagle, laugh like a kookaburra, love like a dove, be as good as a goose, and proud as a peacock... and he and they realized, he had become...one perfect parrot!

"I shall the effect of this good lesson

keep as watchman to my heart."

William Shakespeare

Chapter 10: Lessons Learned

There are many lessons to be learned from Meedy the parrot.

He was a young parrot headed for success until he allowed the sour advice from his father (a once principled and kind man – now gone rogue) and others to influence him in ways that influenced his leadership ability both towards himself and others. From The No Good Leader, we learnt that:

I.   As a leader, you should be careful about advice and instruction you receive into your heart for it can change your perception of the world and life, for better or worse.

II.   Regardless how well liked you are in an organization, one critically wrong move and you're gone! So conduct yourself with respect and treat others professionally and kindly as you would like to be treated. Obey the golden rule.

III. Despite mistakes you have made in the past, there is hope while there is life, so never ever give up! Keep on learning more about self-leadership and keep on aspiring to greater heights. Keep on moving full speed ahead towards your goal. Realign your target where necessary and with persistence, polish and perfection you will succeed!

IV.   Make right any wrongs, seek forgiveness from those you may have wronged and move on towards your destination of peace and success.

V.   Mentoring is essential. Where would Meedy have been without Colonel? He would have probably wound up worse than he had ever been. Sometimes it takes one's being in the lowest of lows to find answers to life's problems. Sometimes being in a down-and-out situation such as Meedy was (having fallen from grace to grass) could be a blessing in disguise...if only we don't stop asking ourselves the right analytical questions, being hopeful and optimistic that things can and will change as we deliberately take massive action.

VI. There is power in having a great mentor or coach to guide you towards your goals and dreams. Surround yourself with great forward-thinking people and develop an inner-circle (or mastermind alliance) to assist you and guide you towards your definite chief aim. If you do not have a mentor or a coach, find one! Get plugged into to a system that offers you guidance consistently. Find a coach who will hold you accountable and consistently work with you towards your definite chief aim.

VII. Pay the price for success. Spend time and resources to constantly grow in your field of expertise towards your expanding dreams. Take deliberate growth steps towards being the "best you" there could ever be. Become the "real you" who constantly maximizes your full potential.

About the Trainer

Phill C. Akinwale, PMP has managed projects and operational endeavors across government and private sectors, in various companies including Motorola, Honeywell, Emerson, Skillsoft, Citigroup, Iron Mountain, Brown and Caldwell and US Airways. With vast experience in different facets of project management and rigorous project controls, he has trained employees and project managers on business management tools and project management.

He has mentored and trained hundreds of project managers to success on the PMP® exam. A strong advocate of doing things according to a deliberate process approach, his training approach emphasizes the importance of putting structure around processes. As a co-founder of Praizion Media, a PMI Registered Education Provider (R.E.P), Phill continues to contribute to project management education through live training, audio training materials and several publications for PMP exam preparation.

As a John Maxwell Certified Coach, Teacher and Speaker, Phill offers workshops, seminars, keynote speaking, and coaching, aiding your personal and professional growth through study and practical application of John Maxwell's proven leadership methods. Working together, Phill will move you and your team or organization in the desired direction to reach your goals.

Visit *www.praizion.com* or *www.leadershipstreet.com*